GERMANY BY TRAIN TRAVEL GUIDE 2025-2026

BY

Rune Greyhound

A Note to Our Readers

Welcome, fellow traveler! Before we plunge into this guide, I wanted to take a moment to address something important: while you won't find any images or maps included here, rest assured that every effort has been made to provide vivid descriptions and helpful information to bring your journey to life. Think of this as an invitation to explore with your imagination—and perhaps even discover new perspectives along the way.

My goal is simple: to equip you with everything you need to create unforgettable experiences on your travels, tailored to your own unique interests and preferences. Whether you're seeking hidden gems, cultural insights, or practical tips, my hope is that you'll find inspiration within these pages to craft adventures that resonate deeply with you.

Table of Contents

Acknowledgments

Writing this book has been a journey of its own, much like the train rides it celebrates. While the words on these pages are mine, they would not have come to life without the support, encouragement, and expertise of so many wonderful individuals along the way. To each of you, I extend my deepest gratitude.

First and foremost, I want to thank the travelers who shared their stories, insights, and photographs—your experiences breathe life into this guide. Your passion for exploring Germany by train reminds us all why travel is such a transformative and enriching part of our lives. Thank you for allowing me to weave your voices into this narrative.

A special thanks goes to the team at Deutsche Bahn (DB) and other rail enthusiasts who patiently answered my countless questions about schedules, ticketing systems, and regional routes. Your dedication to making train travel accessible and efficient inspires both travelers and writers alike.

I'm also deeply grateful to the local guides, historians, and cultural experts who helped verify facts and provided context about Germany's rich history, vibrant cities, and stunning landscapes. Your knowledge ensured that this guide remains accurate, engaging, and respectful of the country's traditions.

To my family and friends, thank you for believing in this project from the very beginning. Your unwavering support kept me motivated during late-night writing sessions and moments of self-doubt. Special mention goes to [insert names if applicable], whose curiosity about Germany fueled many spirited discussions and ideas.

This book would not be complete without acknowledging the incredible editors, designers, and publishers who brought it to life. From refining the language to creating visually appealing maps and layouts, your hard work transformed a rough draft into a polished guidebook. Thank you for helping me realize my vision.

Lastly, I owe immense gratitude to you, dear reader. By choosing this book as your companion for exploring Germany by train, you've made all the effort worthwhile. It's my hope that this guide empowers you to commence on adventures with confidence, curiosity, and joy.

As trains crisscross Germany, connecting people and places, so too do books connect writers and readers across time and space. I am humbled and honored to share this ride with you. Here's to new journeys, shared stories, and the magic of discovery.

Thank you—all aboard!

Dedication

This book is dedicated to the curious souls who believe that every journey holds the promise of discovery.

To those who have ever gazed out of a train window, watching the world blur by in a kaleidoscope of landscapes, cultures, and stories—this is for you. May your travels inspire wonder, spark connections, and remind you of the beauty that lies both within and beyond the rails.

It is also a tribute to Germany—a country whose rich history, vibrant cities, and breathtaking scenery continue to captivate hearts around the globe. From its medieval castles to its modern metropolises, Germany has long been a beacon of resilience, creativity, and unity. This guide seeks to honor its spirit by inviting readers to explore its treasures in the most sustainable and immersive way possible: by train.

Finally, I dedicate this book to anyone who has ever felt the pull of adventure but hesitated to take the first step. Let these pages be your compass, your ticket, and your companion as you commence on your own unforgettable journey through Germany's heart and soul.

May your tracks lead you to new horizons, and may your memories carry you home.
To all travelers—you are the true authors of this story.

Happy trails, and safe journeys.

Chapter 1: Introduction

Welcome to the beginning of your journey through Germany by train! Whether you're dreaming of exploring medieval castles, sipping wine along scenic rivers, or strolling through vibrant cities, this guide is here to help you plan and enjoy every moment. Let's plunge in!

1.1 Welcome to Germany by Train

Germany is a country rich in history, culture, and natural beauty—and there's no better way to experience it than by train. Imagine gliding past rolling hills, charming villages, and bustling metropolises while sipping coffee and gazing out at breathtaking views. Sounds magical, right? That's exactly what awaits you on this adventure.

This guide is designed for first-time travelers who want to explore Germany without stress. We'll cover everything from booking tickets to navigating train stations, so you can focus on enjoying your trip. By the end of this chapter, you'll understand why traveling by train is not just convenient but also one of the most rewarding ways to see Germany.

1.2 Why Travel by Train in Germany?

Germany's rail network is among the best in the world, making trains an ideal choice for travelers. Here are some reasons why:

Convenience
Trains connect nearly every corner of the country, from big cities like Berlin and Munich to small towns tucked away in the countryside. With frequent departures and high-speed options, you won't waste time waiting around.

Scenic Views
Unlike flying or driving, train travel lets you relax and soak up the scenery. From vineyard-lined valleys to snow-capped mountains, you'll get front-row seats to Germany's stunning landscapes.

Eco-Friendly Travel
If you care about the environment, trains are a green alternative to cars and planes. They produce far fewer

emissions per passenger, helping you reduce your carbon footprint while still having an amazing trip.

Ease of Use
German trains are known for their punctuality and efficiency. Even if you've never taken a train before, don't worry—we'll walk you through every step of the process.

Cost-Effectiveness
While some routes can be pricey, many offer affordable options, especially if you book early or use discount passes like the German Rail Pass or Bahncard. Plus, you save money by skipping rental cars and gas fees.

By choosing trains, you're opting for a hassle-free, sustainable, and unforgettable way to discover Germany.

1.3 History of Germany

To truly appreciate Germany, it helps to know a bit about its fascinating history. Germany has been shaped by centuries of innovation, conflict, and resilience.

- Ancient Beginnings: The region now known as Germany was home to Celtic and Germanic tribes long before recorded history.
- The Holy Roman Empire (800–1806): This vast empire laid the foundation for modern Europe, with power centered in what is now Germany.
- World Wars and Division: Two devastating World Wars led to Germany's division into East and West after 1945. The Berlin Wall became a symbol of this split during the Cold War.
- Reunification (1990): After decades apart, East and West Germany reunited peacefully in 1990, marking a new era of unity and progress.

Today, Germany is a global leader in technology, industry, and sustainability, blending its historic roots with forward-thinking innovation. As you travel, you'll encounter reminders of this complex past—from ancient castles to modern skyscrapers.

1.4 History of Germany's Rail System

Germany's love affair with trains began in the 19th century, and the rail system has played a key role in shaping the nation ever since.

- The First Trains (1835): Germany's first railway line opened between Nuremberg and Fürth, sparking a transportation revolution.
- Expansion Across the Country: Over the next century, railways spread rapidly, connecting cities and boosting trade and tourism.
- Post-War Reconstruction: After WWII, rebuilding the rail network was crucial to reconnecting East and West Germany.
- Modern Innovations: Today, Germany boasts one of the fastest and most advanced rail systems in the world, thanks to high-speed ICE (InterCity Express) trains that zip across the country at speeds up to 300 km/h (186 mph).

Deutsche Bahn (DB), the national railway company, operates most of Germany's trains. While delays occasionally happen, DB is renowned for its reliability and commitment to improving services.

1.5 Weather and Climate

Germany's weather varies depending on where you go, but overall, it has a temperate climate with four distinct seasons. Knowing what to expect will help you pack appropriately.

- Spring (March–May): Mild temperatures and blooming flowers make spring a lovely time to visit. Expect highs of 10–20°C (50–68°F).
- Summer (June–August): Warm and sunny, with occasional rain showers. Temperatures range from 20–30°C (68–86°F).
- Autumn (September–November): Cooler weather and colorful foliage create a cozy atmosphere. Highs drop to 10–15°C (50–59°F).
- Winter (December–February): Cold and sometimes snowy, especially in the south. Temperatures hover between -5°C and 5°C (23–41°F).

Tip: Pack layers! Germany's weather can change quickly, so being prepared is key.

1.6 Currency and Money Matters

Germany uses the Euro (€) as its currency, which makes budgeting straightforward if you're coming from another Eurozone country. If not, here's what you need to know:

- Cash vs. Cards: While credit cards are widely accepted, smaller shops and rural areas may only take cash. It's always good to carry some Euros with you.

-ATMs: You'll find ATMs (called "Geldautomaten") everywhere. Look for major banks like Deutsche Bank or Sparkasse for lower fees.

- Tipping: Tipping is customary in restaurants and cafes. Round up your bill or leave 5–10% for good service.

-Budgeting Tips: Trains, food, and accommodations vary in price, but Germany offers plenty of affordable options. For example, street food like currywurst is cheap and delicious!

Pro Tip: Notify your bank before traveling to avoid issues with international transactions.

1.7 How This Guide Will Help You

Traveling to a new country can feel overwhelming, but this guide is here to simplify things. Here's how we'll help:

- Step-by-Step Instructions: From buying tickets to finding your platform, we break down each part of train travel into easy-to-follow steps.

- Practical Advice: Learn insider tips on saving money, avoiding common mistakes, and staying safe on the road.
- Inspiration: Discover must-see destinations, hidden gems, and unique experiences tailored to different types of travelers.
- Flexibility: Whether you prefer planning every detail or winging it, this guide adapts to your style.

By the time you finish reading, you'll feel confident and excited to hop aboard a train and start exploring Germany. So grab your suitcase, pick your route, and let the adventure begin.

Chapter 2: Getting Started

Now that you're excited about exploring Germany by train, let's plunge into the basics of how the rail system works. This chapter will give you a clear understanding of the different types of trains, how to read schedules, and essential vocabulary to make your journey smooth and stress-free. By the end, you'll feel like a pro navigating Germany's rails!

2.1 Understanding the German Rail System

Germany's rail network is one of the most efficient and extensive in the world, operated primarily by Deutsche Bahn (DB), the national railway company. Think of it as the backbone of travel in Germany—it connects nearly every city, town, and village, making it easy to explore even remote areas.

Here's what makes the system so great:
- Coverage: Trains go everywhere, from bustling metropolises like Berlin and Munich to quaint villages nestled in the Black Forest.

- Speed: High-speed trains like the ICE can take you across the country in just a few hours.
-Reliability: While delays happen occasionally, German trains are known for being punctual.
- Comfort: Modern amenities like Wi-Fi, power outlets, and spacious seating make long journeys enjoyable.

The key to mastering train travel in Germany is knowing which type of train suits your needs. That's where the next section comes in!

2.2 Types of Trains: ICE, IC, RE, and S-Bahn Explained

Germany has several types of trains, each designed for different purposes. Don't worry—they're easier to understand than they sound. Here's a breakdown:

ICE (InterCity Express)
- What It Is: The fastest and most luxurious option.
- Speed: Up to 300 km/h (186 mph).
- Where It Goes: Major cities like Berlin, Hamburg, Frankfurt, Cologne, and Munich.
- Best For: Long-distance travel when time is important.

- Pro Tip: Reserve seats in advance to guarantee a spot on busy routes.

IC (InterCity)
- What It Is: Similar to the ICE but slightly slower and less frequent.
- Speed: Around 200 km/h (124 mph).
- Where It Goes: Connects larger cities and some regional hubs.
- Best For: Travelers who want comfort without paying top dollar for an ICE ticket.

RE (Regional Express) & RB (Regionalbahn)
- What It Is: Slower regional trains that stop at smaller towns and stations.
- Speed: Much slower than ICE or IC, but still reliable.
- Where It Goes: Perfect for reaching scenic countryside spots, castles, and off-the-beaten-path destinations.
- Best For: Shorter trips or exploring rural areas.
- Pro Tip: These trains don't require seat reservations, so they're more flexible.

S-Bahn (Stadtschnellbahn)
- What It Is: Suburban commuter trains found in metropolitan areas.
- Speed: Slowest of all, but convenient for getting around cities.

- Where It Goes: Within and between suburbs of major cities like Berlin, Munich, and Hamburg.
- Best For: Day trips from city centers to nearby attractions.

Quick Summary Table:

Train Type	Speed	Stops	Best Use Case
ICE	Very Fast	Few	Long-distance city-to-city
IC	Fast	Moderate	City connections
RE/RB	Slow-Medium	Many	Rural exploration
S-Bahn	Slow	Very Frequent	Urban/suburban commuting

Understanding these differences will help you choose the right train for your itinerary.

2.3 How to Read Train Schedules

Reading train schedules might seem intimidating at first, but once you know what to look for, it's simple. Here's a step-by-step guide:

Step 1: Find Your Route
Use tools like the **DB Navigator** app or websites like bahn.com to search for your route. Enter your departure point, destination, and desired time.

Step 2: Understand the Timetable
Once you've found your train, you'll see details like:
- Departure Time: When the train leaves your starting station.
- Arrival Time: When it arrives at your destination.
- Platform Number: Where to board the train (this may change, so always check screens before boarding).
- Duration: Total travel time.
- Train Type: ICE, IC, RE, etc.

Example Schedule Entry:

Berlin Hbf → Munich Hbf
Train: ICE 1234
Departs: 08:00 | Arrives: 12:30
Duration: 4h 30m
Platform: 11

Step 3: Look for Connections

If your journey requires transferring trains, the schedule will show connection times. Make sure you have enough time to switch platforms—usually 5–15 minutes is sufficient.

Step 4: Check Real-Time Updates
Trains often run on time, but delays happen. Use the DB app or digital signs at stations to stay updated.

Pro Tips:
- Always arrive at least 10 minutes early for long-distance trains (ICE/IC).
- Confirm platform numbers shortly before departure, as last-minute changes occur.

2.4 Essential Vocabulary for Train Travel

Knowing a few key German words and phrases will boost your confidence when navigating the rail system. Here's a handy list:

Basic Words
- Zug – Train
- Bahnhof – Train station
- Gleis – Platform
- Fahrplan – Timetable/Schedule
- Ticket – Ticket

At the Station
- Wo ist der Fahrkartenautomat? – Where is the ticket machine?
- Welches Gleis für [Destination]? – Which platform for [destination]?
- Entschuldigung, wo geht es zu Gleis X? – Excuse me, where is platform X?

Onboard
- Reserviert – Reserved (seat)
- Frei – Free (unreserved seat)
- Toilette – Toilet/Bathroom
- Notausgang – Emergency exit

Helpful Phrases
- Ich habe eine Frage. – I have a question.
- Wie lange dauert die Fahrt? – How long does the ride take?
- Wann kommen wir an? – When do we arrive?
- Können Sie mir helfen? – Can you help me?

Even if you only remember a couple of these, locals will appreciate your effort—and many Germans speak excellent English, so don't hesitate to ask for clarification.

With this knowledge under your belt, you're ready to tackle the German rail system like a pro.

Chapter 3: Planning Your Journey

Planning your trip is where the excitement begins! This chapter will guide you through choosing destinations, creating an itinerary, and preparing for your adventure. We'll also provide sample itineraries to inspire your travels and practical tips for packing and connecting from neighboring countries.

3.1 Choosing Your Destinations: Top Cities and Attractions

Germany offers a mix of vibrant cities, charming small towns, and breathtaking natural landscapes. Here are some must-visit destinations:

Big Cities You Can't Miss
- Berlin: Germany's capital is a hub of history, culture, and nightlife. Visit the Brandenburg Gate, Berlin Wall Memorial, Museum Island, and trendy neighborhoods like Kreuzberg.

- Munich: The heart of Bavaria, Munich combines tradition with modernity. Explore Marienplatz, Nymphenburg Palace, and the world-famous Oktoberfest (if visiting in autumn).
-Hamburg: Known for its port, Elbphilharmonie concert hall, and lively Reeperbahn district. Don't miss a harbor boat tour!
- Cologne: Famous for its stunning cathedral (Kölner Dom), Romanesque churches, and vibrant arts scene along the Rhine River.
- Frankfurt: A financial powerhouse with a charming old town, skyscrapers, and proximity to the Rhine Valley.

Hidden Gems and Smaller Towns
- Heidelberg: A romantic university town with a picturesque castle overlooking the Neckar River.
- Rothenburg ob der Tauber: A fairytale medieval town frozen in time.
- Freiburg: Nestled near the Black Forest, this sunny city is perfect for eco-friendly travelers.
- Dresden: Rebuilt after WWII, Dresden boasts Baroque architecture and museums.
- Bamberg: A UNESCO World Heritage Site with cobblestone streets and delicious smoked beer.

Natural Wonders

- Black Forest: Hike, bike, or simply soak in the serene beauty of Germany's iconic woodland region.
- Rhine Valley: Cruise past castles, vineyards, and quaint villages.
- Bavarian Alps: Stunning peaks and lakes, including Lake Constance and King Ludwig II's fairy-tale castles.
- Saxon Switzerland National Park: Dramatic sandstone formations and hiking trails.

Pick destinations that align with your interests—whether it's history, food, nature, or urban exploration.

3.2 Creating Your Itinerary: Suggested Routes and Duration

A well-planned itinerary ensures you make the most of your trip. Below are two popular route ideas based on travel duration:

Short Trip (7 Days)
Route: Berlin → Dresden → Leipzig → Frankfurt → Cologne
Highlights:

- Start in Berlin to explore its rich history and vibrant arts scene.
- Head to Dresden for Baroque architecture and cultural treasures.
- Stop in Leipzig, known for its music heritage and creative vibe.
- Travel to Frankfurt for modern skyscrapers and nearby wine regions.
- End in Cologne to see the cathedral and enjoy riverside views.

Longer Adventure (14 Days)
Route: Munich → Salzburg → Neuschwanstein Castle → Stuttgart → Heidelberg → Rhine Valley → Hamburg
Highlights:
- Begin in Munich for Bavarian charm and beer gardens.
- Cross into Austria to visit Salzburg, Mozart's birthplace.
- Return to Germany to marvel at Neuschwanstein Castle.
- Explore Stuttgart's automotive museums and vineyards.
- Wander through Heidelberg's historic streets.
- Cruise the Rhine Valley and admire its castles.
- Finish in Hamburg for maritime adventures.

Feel free to adjust these routes based on your preferences!

3.3 Seasonal Considerations: Best Times to Travel

The best time to visit depends on what kind of experience you're looking for:

Spring (March–May):
- Pros: Mild weather, blooming flowers, fewer tourists.
- Cons: Some mountain attractions may still be closed due to snow.

Summer (June–August):
- Pros: Warm weather, outdoor festivals, extended daylight hours.
- Cons: Peak tourist season means higher prices and crowded trains.

Autumn (September–November):
- Pros: Cooler temperatures, fall foliage, harvest festivals like Oktoberfest.
- Cons: Weather becomes unpredictable toward November.

Winter (December–February):
- Pros: Christmas markets, skiing in the Alps, cozy atmosphere.
- Cons: Cold weather and potential train delays due to snow.

For budget-conscious travelers, spring and autumn offer the best balance of pleasant weather and affordable rates.

3.4 How to Connect From Neighboring Countries

Germany's central location makes it easy to connect from other European nations by train. Here's how:

From France
- Take the high-speed TGV or ICE trains from Paris to Frankfurt, Stuttgart, or Munich.
- Example Route: Paris → Strasbourg → Karlsruhe → Stuttgart.

From Belgium/Netherlands
- Direct ICE trains link Brussels and Amsterdam to Cologne, Düsseldorf, and beyond.

- Example Route: Amsterdam → Duisburg → Cologne.

From Switzerland
- Swiss Federal Railways (SBB) connects seamlessly with German trains via Basel or Freiburg.
- Example Route: Zurich → Stuttgart → Munich.

From Austria
- Cross-border routes connect Vienna, Salzburg, and Innsbruck to Munich and beyond.
- Example Route: Vienna → Passau → Regensburg → Nuremberg.

From Poland/Czech Republic
- Regional and international trains link Prague, Krakow, and Warsaw to Dresden, Berlin, and Frankfurt.
- Example Route: Prague → Dresden → Leipzig.

Pro Tip: Use the Eurail Pass if you plan to hop between multiple countries—it's cost-effective and flexible.

3.5 Packing Essentials: What to Bring and What Not to Bring

Packing smart is crucial for comfortable train travel. Here's a checklist:

What to Bring
- Clothing: Layers for changing weather; sturdy shoes for walking.
- Travel Documents: Passport, tickets, printed confirmations, and any necessary visas.
- Tech Gear: Phone charger, portable power bank, headphones.
- Snacks & Water Bottle: For long journeys.
-Entertainment: Books, e-readers, or downloaded movies/shows.
- Daypack: For carrying essentials during day trips.

What Not to Bring
- Heavy Luggage: Stick to one suitcase and a carry-on to avoid hassle.
- Valuables: Leave expensive jewelry at home; keep electronics secure.
- Too Many Shoes: Pack versatile footwear instead of multiple pairs.

Bonus Tip: Always label your luggage clearly in case it gets misplaced.

3.6 Sample Itineraries: 7-Day and 14-Day Plans

7-Day Itinerary: Classic Highlights
Day 1: Arrive in Berlin – Explore Brandenburg Gate and Museum Island.
Day 2: Day trip to Potsdam – Visit Sanssouci Palace.
Day 3: Train to Dresden – Discover Zwinger Palace and Frauenkirche.
Day 4: Travel to Leipzig – Enjoy musical landmarks and street art.
Day 5: Head to Frankfurt – Climb the Main Tower for panoramic views.
Day 6: Day trip to Rhine Valley – Wine tasting and castle tours.
Day 7: End in Cologne – Admire Kölner Dom before departure.

14-Day Itinerary: Deep plunge into Germany
Day 1–2: Munich – Beer gardens, English Garden, BMW Museum.
Day 3: Day trip to Neuschwanstein Castle – Fairy-tale vibes.

Day 4–5: Stuttgart – Mercedes-Benz Museum, vineyard visits.

Day 6–7: Heidelberg – Romantic ruins and student life.

Day 8–9: Rhine Valley – Castles, cruises, and Riesling tastings.

Day 10–11: Hamburg – Harbor tours, Miniatur Wunderland.

Day 12–13: Berlin – History, nightlife, and street food.

Day 14: Departure – Reflect on your incredible journey.

With these tools and inspiration, you're ready to craft your dream itinerary.

Chapter 4: Tickets and Pricing

Buying train tickets in Germany doesn't have to be complicated. This chapter will guide you through the process, explain different ticket types, and show you how to save money with passes and discounts. By the end, you'll know exactly how to secure the best deals for your journey.

4.1 How to Buy Train Tickets: Online vs. At the Station

There are two main ways to purchase train tickets in Germany: online or at the station. Each method has its pros and cons, so let's break them down.

Buying Tickets Online
- Pros:
- Convenient: You can book from anywhere using your phone, tablet, or computer.

- Early-bird discounts: Booking ahead often gets you cheaper fares.
- Easier to compare options: Use tools like DB Navigator to find the best routes and prices.
- Cons:
- Requires planning: You need internet access and time to research schedules.
- Printing or downloading: Some tickets must be printed or shown on a smartphone.

Steps to Buy Online:
1. Visit [bahn.com](https://www.bahn.com) or download the DB Navigator app.
2. Enter your departure point, destination, and travel dates/times.
3. Select your preferred train and class (e.g., Economy or First Class).
4. Pay securely and receive your e-ticket via email or the app.

Buying Tickets at the Station
- Pros:
- No advance planning needed: Perfect for spontaneous travelers.
- Assistance available: Staffed counters can help if you're unsure about routes or payment.
- Cons:

- Higher prices: Last-minute tickets bought at the station are usually more expensive.
- Long lines: Popular stations can get crowded, especially during peak hours.

Steps to Buy at the Station:
1. Use automated ticket machines (available in multiple languages).
- Select "English" if you're not comfortable with German.
- Follow prompts to choose your route and ticket type.
2. Alternatively, visit the service counter for personalized assistance.
3. Pay with cash, card, or contactless methods.

Pro Tip: If you're buying at the station, arrive at least 15–20 minutes before departure to avoid stress.

4.2 Understanding Ticket Types: Single, Round Trip, and More

Germany offers a variety of ticket types to suit different needs. Here's what you need to know:

Single Tickets
- For one-way trips between two points.

- Ideal for short journeys or when you don't plan to return immediately.

Round-Trip Tickets
- Covers both directions of a trip (outbound and inbound).
- Often slightly cheaper than buying two separate single tickets.

Group Tickets
-Schönes-Wochenende-Ticket (Happy Weekend Ticket): Valid for up to 5 people traveling together on regional trains (RE/RB) all day Saturday or Sunday. Great for budget-conscious groups!
-Quer-durchs-Land-Ticket (Across-the-Country Ticket): Similar to the weekend ticket but valid Monday–Friday for regional trains nationwide.

Flexpreis vs. Sparpreis
- Flexpreis (Flexible Fare): Fully refundable and allows changes without fees. Best for last-minute bookings.
-Sparpreis (Saver Fare): Cheaper but non-refundable; requires advance booking. Limited seats available per train.

First Class vs. Second Class

- Second Class: Standard seating; perfectly comfortable for most travelers.
Available
- First Class: Spacious seats, quieter cars, and complimentary snacks/beverages on some long-distance trains. Worth considering for luxury seekers.

Pro Tip: Always check whether your ticket includes seat reservations. On high-speed trains like ICE, reserved seats ensure a guaranteed spot.

4.3 Passes and Discounts: The German Rail Pass Explained

If you're planning an extended stay or visiting multiple cities, rail passes and discounts can save you significant money. Here's an overview:

German Rail Pass
- What It Is: A flexible pass that allows unlimited travel on Deutsche Bahn trains within a set number of days.
- Who It's For: Tourists visiting Germany for a limited time.

- How It Works: Choose between 3, 4, 5, 7, or 10 travel days within a one-month period. Travel days can be used consecutively or spread out.
- Cost: Prices vary depending on the number of days and class (Economy or First Class).

Example:
- A 7-day pass might cost around €250–€300 for second-class travel.
- Activating the pass is simple—just write the date on it before boarding your first train.

Note: The German Rail Pass covers regional and long-distance trains but does not include seat reservations, which may still need to be purchased separately.

Bahncard Discounts
- Bahncard 25: Offers 25% off standard fares for three months (€62) or a year (€255).
- Bahncard 50: Provides 50% off fares for a year (€255). Best for frequent travelers.
- These cards pay for themselves quickly if you take several long-distance trips.

Other Discounts
- Youth Discount: Travelers under 27 get reduced fares on many tickets.

- Group Discounts: Save money by traveling with friends or family (e.g., Schönes-Wochenende-Ticket).
- Regional Specials: Look for discounted tickets specific to certain areas, such as Bayern-Ticket or Baden-Württemberg-Ticket.

Pro Tip: Combine a rail pass with regional specials for maximum savings.

4.4 When to Book: Tips for Getting the Best Deals

Timing is everything when it comes to saving money on train tickets. Follow these tips to score the cheapest fares:

Book Early
- Deutsche Bahn releases discounted Sparpreis tickets up to 180 days in advance.
- The earlier you book, the better chance you have of snagging low-cost options.

Travel Off-Peak
- Avoid peak hours (weekdays 6–9 AM and 4–7 PM) when fares are highest.

- Midday and late-night trains often offer cheaper rates.

Be Flexible
- Consider traveling on less popular days (e.g., Tuesdays or Wednesdays) instead of weekends.
- Overnight trains can also provide unique experiences at lower costs.

Use Apps and Alerts
- Download the DB Navigator app to track price drops and receive notifications about sales.
- Third-party websites like Omio or Trainline sometimes offer competitive pricing.

Leverage Group Discounts
- If traveling with others, opt for group tickets like the Schönes-Wochenende-Ticket or Quer-durchs-Land-Ticket.

Look for Promotions
- Keep an eye out for seasonal promotions, flash sales, or special event discounts.

Final Tip: Always double-check your booking details after purchasing to ensure accuracy. Mistakes happen, and catching errors early can prevent headaches later.

With this knowledge, you're equipped to navigate the world of German train tickets like a pro.

Chapter 5: Navigating Train Stations

Train stations in Germany are bustling hubs of activity, but they're also designed to be traveler-friendly. Whether you're stepping into a grand historic station like Berlin Hauptbahnhof or a smaller regional stop, knowing how to navigate them efficiently will make your journey smoother. Let's explore everything you need to know about major stations, facilities, finding your platform, and staying safe.

5.1 Major Train Stations: Berlin, Munich, Frankfurt & More

Germany is home to some of the most impressive train stations in Europe, many of which serve as key transit points for travelers. Here's a quick overview of the biggest and busiest ones:

Berlin Hauptbahnhof (Central Station)

-Why It Matters: The largest and most modern train station in Europe, connecting long-distance, regional, and S-Bahn trains.

-Highlights: A stunning glass-and-steel structure with shops, restaurants, and easy access to public transport.

- Pro Tip: Look for signs pointing to "Hbf" (short for Hauptbahnhof) on maps—it's often a central meeting point.

Munich Hauptbahnhof

- Why It Matters: The gateway to Bavaria, offering connections to Austria, Switzerland, and southern Germany.

- Highlights: Beautiful architecture, a wide range of amenities, and proximity to Marienplatz.

- Pro Tip: Arrive early to enjoy coffee at one of the station's cozy cafés.

Frankfurt Hauptbahnhof

- Why It Matters: One of the busiest stations in Germany, serving as a hub for international and domestic travel.

- Highlights: Direct links to Frankfurt Airport via the ICE train; plenty of dining and shopping options.

- Pro Tip: Use the station's free Wi-Fi while waiting for your train.

Cologne Hauptbahnhof

- Why It Matters: Located next to Cologne Cathedral, this station offers breathtaking views and convenient access to the city center.
- Highlights: Art installations and a lively atmosphere thanks to its location near tourist attractions.
- Pro Tip: Take a moment to snap photos of the cathedral before boarding your train.

Hamburg Hauptbahnhof
- Why It Matters: Northern Germany's main transport hub, linking cities like Copenhagen and Berlin.
- Highlights: Clean facilities, helpful staff, and an abundance of bakeries selling fresh pretzels.
- Pro Tip: Explore the station's upper levels for panoramic views of the surrounding area.

These stations are well-equipped to handle millions of passengers annually, so even if they seem overwhelming at first, you'll quickly adapt once you understand their layout.

5.2 Facilities and Services at Stations: What to Expect

German train stations are more than just places to catch a train—they're mini-cities with all the essentials. Here's what you can expect:

Basic Amenities
- Ticket Counters and Machines: Available in multiple languages for purchasing tickets.
- Restrooms: Clean and accessible, though some charge a small fee (€0.50–€1).
- Luggage Lockers: Secure storage for bags if you have time between connections.
- Lost & Found Offices: If you misplace something, report it here.

Food and Drink
- Cafés and Bakeries: Perfect for grabbing a quick coffee or pastry.
- Fast-Food Chains: McDonald's, Burger King, and local favorites like Nordsee (seafood) are common.
- Sit-Down Restaurants: Larger stations often have full-service eateries for leisurely meals.

Shopping
- Newsstands and Convenience Stores: Stock up on snacks, magazines, and toiletries.
- Fashion and Electronics Shops: Ideal for last-minute purchases or souvenirs.

Additional Services
- Travel Information Desks: Staffed by multilingual agents who can answer questions.
- Pharmacies and First Aid: Available in larger stations for emergencies.
- Wi-Fi and Charging Stations: Stay connected while you wait.

Pro Tip: Many stations host Christmas markets during winter—don't miss these festive pop-ups!

5.3 Finding Your Platform: A Step-by-Step Guide

Finding your platform might seem daunting at first, but German stations are designed to guide you clearly. Follow these steps:

Step 1: Locate Departure Boards
- Head to the large digital screens displaying departure times, destinations, and platforms.
- Columns to look for:
- Zug nach (Train to): Destination.
- Abfahrt (Departure): Scheduled departure time.
- Gleis (Platform): Assigned platform number.

Step 2: Match Your Ticket Details
- Check your ticket or app confirmation to confirm your train number (e.g., ICE 1234) and destination.
- Cross-reference this info with the departure board to find your platform.

Step 3: Follow Signage
- Once you know your platform, follow overhead signs labeled with numbers (e.g., "Gleis 7").
- Escalators, elevators, and stairs will lead you to the correct level.

Step 4: Double-Check Before Boarding
- Platforms sometimes change last minute, especially in busy stations. Keep an eye on announcements and updated screens.
- Confirm your train car by checking the display above each section—it shows the final destination and stops along the way.

Pro Tip: Arrive at least 10 minutes early for long-distance trains (ICE/IC) to avoid stress.

5.4 Safety Tips and Etiquette in Stations

While German train stations are generally safe, it's always wise to stay alert and respectful. Here's how to ensure a smooth experience:

Safety Tips
- Keep Valuables Secure: Avoid flashy jewelry and keep wallets, phones, and passports close to your body.
- Watch for Scams: Be cautious of overly friendly strangers asking for help or unsolicited offers.
- Stick to Well-Lit Areas: Especially late at night, stick to busier parts of the station where staff and security are present.
- Report Suspicious Activity: Contact station personnel or call emergency services (110 for police) if needed.

Etiquette Guidelines
- Respect Queues: Germans value order, so always line up neatly when buying tickets or boarding trains.
-Keep Noise Levels Down: Loud conversations or music can disturb others, particularly in quieter areas.
- Dispose of Trash Properly: Recycling bins are clearly marked—use them responsibly.
- Give Priority Seating: In waiting areas, offer seats to elderly, pregnant, or disabled individuals.

Accessibility Considerations

- Most major stations are wheelchair-friendly, with ramps, elevators, and tactile paving for visually impaired travelers.
- Service animals are welcome, and assistance can be arranged in advance through Deutsche Bahn.

Final Thought: Treat train stations as shared spaces. Being considerate ensures everyone has a pleasant experience.

By now, you should feel confident navigating any German train station, no matter how big or busy.

Chapter 6: Exploring Major Cities by Train

Germany's cities are vibrant, diverse, and full of character—each offering a unique experience. Thanks to the country's excellent rail network, getting between these urban gems is easy, fast, and scenic. In this chapter, we'll explore some of Germany's most iconic cities, including how to reach them by train and what makes each one special.

6.1 Berlin: A City of History and Culture

How to Get There by Train:
Berlin Hauptbahnhof (Central Station) is Germany's largest and most modern train station, making it the primary gateway to the city. High-speed ICE trains connect Berlin to other major cities like Hamburg (1.5 hours), Frankfurt (4–5 hours), Munich (6–7 hours), and Cologne (4–5 hours). Regional trains also link Berlin to nearby destinations such as Potsdam (30 minutes) and Leipzig (1 hour).

Why Visit Berlin?

- History Comes Alive: Walk through Checkpoint Charlie, visit the Berlin Wall Memorial, and explore Museum Island.
- Iconic Landmarks: Admire the Brandenburg Gate, Reichstag Building, and East Side Gallery.
- Vibrant Arts Scene: Discover street art in Kreuzberg, enjoy performances at the Berlin Philharmonic, or browse galleries in Mitte.
- Nightlife: Berlin is famous for its clubs, bars, and late-night parties.

Must-Do Activities:
- Take a guided walking tour of historical sites.
- Stroll along Unter den Linden boulevard.
- Enjoy currywurst from a street vendor—it's a local favorite!
- Visit Tiergarten Park for a relaxing afternoon.

6.2 Munich: The Heart of Bavaria

How to Get There by Train:
Munich Hauptbahnhof is the main hub for trains arriving from all over Germany and Europe. High-speed ICE trains connect Munich to cities like Frankfurt (3.5 hours), Berlin (6–7 hours), and Stuttgart (2.5 hours). Regional trains also serve

nearby towns like Augsburg (30 minutes), Füssen (2 hours), and Salzburg, Austria (1.5 hours).

Why Visit Munich?
- Bavarian Charm: Experience traditional beer gardens, lederhosen, and Oktoberfest vibes year-round.
- Cultural Treasures: Explore Nymphenburg Palace, BMW Museum, and the Glockenspiel at Marienplatz.
- Outdoor Adventures: Surrounded by the Alps and close to Lake Constance and Neuschwanstein Castle.
- Foodie Heaven: Savor hearty dishes like schnitzel, pretzels, and spätzle.

Must-Do Activities:
- Climb the Alter Peter church tower for panoramic views of the city.
- Relax in the English Garden and watch surfers ride the Eisbach wave.
- Tour the Residenz, the former royal palace.
- Grab a stein of beer at Hofbräuhaus, one of the world's oldest breweries.

6.3 Frankfurt: The Financial Hub and Beyond

How to Get There by Train:
Frankfurt Hauptbahnhof is a major international and domestic hub, served by high-speed ICE trains. It's just 1 hour from Cologne, 2 hours from Stuttgart, and 4–5 hours from Berlin via ICE trains. Frankfurt Airport has its own train station, making it seamless to transfer directly from flights.

Why Visit Frankfurt?
- Skyline Views: Known as "Mainhattan" for its modern skyscrapers, Frankfurt offers stunning cityscapes.
- Rich Heritage: Explore Römer Square, St. Bartholomew's Cathedral, and the Goethe House.
- Wine Country Nearby: Day trips to the Rhine Valley and Rheingau wine region are a must.
- Convenient Base: Frankfurt's central location makes it ideal for exploring other parts of Germany.

Must-Do Activities:
- Ascend the Main Tower for breathtaking views of the city.
- Wander through the Old Town (Altstadt) after recent renovations restored its historic charm.
- Sample local apple cider (Apfelwein) at a traditional tavern.
- Take a river cruise on the Main River.

6.4 Hamburg: Port City Adventures

How to Get There by Train:
Hamburg Hauptbahnhof is well-connected by ICE trains. From Berlin, the trip takes about 2 hours; from Cologne, it's roughly 4 hours. Regional trains link Hamburg to smaller coastal towns like Lübeck (30 minutes) and Cuxhaven (1.5 hours).

Why Visit Hamburg?
-Maritime Spirit: As Germany's second-largest city, Hamburg boasts Europe's third-largest port.
-Architectural Wonders: Visit the Elbphilharmonie concert hall, Speicherstadt warehouse district, and St. Michael's Church.
- Green Spaces: Parks like Planten un Blomen and Alster Lakes make Hamburg feel surprisingly serene.
- Unique Attractions: Miniatur Wunderland, the world's largest model railway, is a highlight.

Must-Do Activities:
- Take a harbor boat tour to see the port up close.
- Explore the Reeperbahn district for nightlife and entertainment.
- Walk along the Elbe River promenade.
- Visit HafenCity, a revitalized waterfront area blending old and new architecture.

6.5 Other Noteworthy Cities: Düsseldorf, Stuttgart & More

Düsseldorf
How to Get There by Train:
Düsseldorf Hauptbahnhof is connected by ICE trains. From Cologne, it's only 20–30 minutes; from Frankfurt, it's about 2 hours.

- Highlights: Fashion capital with luxury shopping on Königsallee, contemporary art museums, and riverside views along the Rhine.
- Must-Do: Try local Altbier at a traditional brewery pub.

Stuttgart
How to Get There by Train:
Stuttgart Hauptbahnhof is served by ICE trains. From Frankfurt, it's a 1-hour ride; from Munich, it's around 2.5 hours.

- Highlights: Home to Mercedes-Benz and Porsche museums, lush vineyards, and Baroque architecture.
- Must-Do: Stroll through Schlossgarten park and visit the Old Castle (Altes Schloss).

Cologne

How to Get There by Train:
Cologne Hauptbahnhof is a key stop on the ICE line. From Düsseldorf, it's just 20 minutes; from Frankfurt, it's about 1 hour.

-Highlights: Kölner Dom (Cologne Cathedral), Romanesque churches, and lively Carnival celebrations.
- Must-Do: Cross the Hohenzollern Bridge and add your own "love lock."

Leipzig
How to Get There by Train:
Leipzig Hauptbahnhof is reachable by ICE trains. From Berlin, it's 1.5 hours; from Dresden, it's about 1 hour.

- Highlights: Known for its music heritage (home to Bach and Mendelssohn), vibrant arts scene, and trendy neighborhoods.
- Must-Do: Visit the Leipzig Market Square and explore the Battle of Nations Monument.

Nuremberg
How to Get There by Train:
Nuremberg Hauptbahnhof is a major stop. From Munich, it's 1 hour; from Frankfurt, it's about 2 hours.

-Highlights: Historic Old Town, Nazi Documentation Center, and Christkindlesmarkt during Christmas.

- Must-Do: Try Nürnberger Bratwurst, a local delicacy.

Pro Tip for Train Travel Between Cities:

- Use apps like DB Navigator or websites like bahn.com to compare routes and prices.

-Consider regional tickets (e.g., Bayern-Ticket, Schönes-Wochenende-Ticket) for affordable day trips within states.

– Reserve seats early for popular routes like Berlin ↔ Munich to guarantee comfort.

By now, you're ready to hop aboard a train and start exploring Germany's incredible cities. Each destination offers something unique, whether it's history, culture, food, or natural beauty.

Chapter 7: Scenic Train Routes

Germany's train network doesn't just connect cities— it also takes you through some of the most breathtaking landscapes in Europe. From rolling hills and medieval castles to snow-capped mountains and vineyard-lined valleys, scenic train routes are a traveler's dream. In this chapter, we'll explore four unforgettable journeys that showcase Germany's natural beauty and cultural treasures.

7.1 The Romantic Road: Cities and Landscapes

Route Highlights:
The Romantic Road is one of Germany's most famous tourist routes, stretching 400 kilometers (250 miles) from Würzburg in the north to Füssen in the south. While much of it is traveled by car or bus, trains provide convenient access to key stops along the way.

How to Experience It by Train:

- Start in Würzburg, accessible via ICE trains from Frankfurt (1 hour). Visit the stunning Würzburg Residence and Marienberg Fortress.
- Take regional trains to Rothenburg ob der Tauber, a fairytale medieval town frozen in time.
- Continue to Augsburg, Bavaria's third-largest city, known for its Renaissance architecture.
- End your journey in Füssen, where you can visit Neuschwanstein Castle—a symbol of Bavarian romance. Trains run regularly between these towns, with connections via Munich.

What to Expect Along the Way:
- Medieval Charm: Rothenburg ob der Tauber feels like stepping into a storybook.
- Baroque Splendor: Würzburg's opulent palace and frescoed ceilings are not to be missed.
- Alpine Views: Near Füssen, enjoy panoramic vistas of the Bavarian Alps.
- Local Cuisine: Try hearty dishes like schweinshaxe (roasted pork knuckle) and käsespätzle (cheesy noodles).

Pro Tip:
Combine train travel with short bus rides or guided tours to fully immerse yourself in the Romantic Road experience.

7.2 Rhine Valley: Vineyards and Castles

Route Highlights:
The Rhine Valley, a UNESCO World Heritage Site, is renowned for its picturesque riverbanks dotted with vineyards, charming villages, and over 40 hilltop castles. This route offers some of the most iconic views in Germany.

How to Experience It by Train:
- Begin in Cologne, easily reachable by ICE trains from Frankfurt (1 hour) or Düsseldorf (30 minutes).
- Board a regional train to Koblenz, where the Rhine and Moselle rivers meet. Don't miss the Deutsches Eck monument.
- Travel further south to Rüdesheim, famous for its wine and the quirky Siegfried's Mechanical Music Cabinet museum.
- End your journey in Mainz, home to Gutenberg Museum and vibrant half-timbered houses.

What to Expect Along the Way:
- Fairytale Castles: Marksburg, Rheinfels, and Burg Eltz are must-see fortresses perched dramatically above the valley.
- Wine Tasting: Sample world-class Rieslings in towns like Bacharach and St. Goar.

- Scenic Cruises: Combine train travel with a leisurely Rhine River cruise for an unforgettable perspective.
- Quaint Villages: Wander cobblestone streets in Boppard, Oberwesel, and Kaub.

Pro Tip:
Look out for the Lorelei Rock—a legendary cliff said to have inspired poets and musicians—between St. Goar and Bacharach.

7.3 The Bavarian Alps: Stunning Mountain Views

Route Highlights:
The Bavarian Alps offer jaw-dropping alpine scenery, crystal-clear lakes, and charming mountain towns. Whether you're a nature lover or seeking tranquility, this route is pure magic.

How to Experience It by Train:
- Start in Munich, accessible via high-speed ICE trains from across Germany.
-Take a regional train to Garmisch-Partenkirchen, a gateway to hiking trails and winter sports.
- Continue to Mittenwald, known for its colorful painted houses and violin-making tradition.

- End your journey at Füssen, near Neuschwanstein and Hohenschwangau castles. Regional trains and buses make it easy to navigate this region.

What to Expect Along the Way:
- Neuschwanstein Castle: King Ludwig II's fairy-tale masterpiece surrounded by dramatic peaks.
- Lake Constance (Bodensee): A serene spot shared by Germany, Austria, and Switzerland.
- Outdoor Adventures: Hike Zugspitze (Germany's highest peak), kayak on Lake Eibsee, or ski in winter.
- Charming Towns: Explore Oberammergau, famous for its Passion Play, and Berchtesgaden, nestled in a national park.

Pro Tip:
Book early during summer and autumn, as these areas attract large crowds eager to see the castles and mountains.

7.4 Hidden Gems: Off-the-Beaten-Path Train Journeys

While popular routes steal the spotlight, Germany has plenty of lesser-known train journeys that reveal hidden treasures. These offbeat destinations are perfect for travelers seeking quieter escapes.

Harz Mountains Narrow-Gauge Railway
- Route Highlights:

This heritage railway winds through the Harz Mountains, offering a nostalgic ride aboard steam-powered trains.

- How to Get There:

Take a train to Wernigerode, the starting point for many narrow-gauge excursions. From Berlin, it's about 2 hours; from Hannover, it's 1.5 hours.

- What to Expect:
- Picturesque forests, deep gorges, and quaint villages.
- Brocken Mountain, the highest peak in the Harz range, often shrouded in mist.
- Local crafts and hearty meals in traditional inns.

Saxon Switzerland National Park
- Route Highlights:

Located near Dresden, this park features dramatic sandstone formations, lush forests, and hiking trails.

- How to Get There:

From Dresden, take a regional train to Bad Schandau, the gateway to the park (about 45 minutes).

- What to Expect:
- Bastei Bridge, a photogenic rock formation overlooking the Elbe River.

- Challenging hikes and peaceful forest walks.
- Riverside cafes serving Saxon specialties like potato soup and quarkkeulchen (potato pancakes).

Black Forest Railway
- Route Highlights:
This scenic line cuts through Germany's iconic Black Forest, famous for cuckoo clocks, dense woodlands, and sparkling lakes.
- How to Get There:
Start in Offenburg or Freiburg, both served by ICE trains. Regional trains then take you deeper into the forest.
- What to Expect:
- Triberg Waterfalls, among the tallest in Germany.
- Traditional farmhouses and cozy guesthouses.
- Black Forest cake and smoked ham straight from local producers.

Pro Tip:
These hidden gems are best explored outside peak tourist seasons (spring or fall), when you can savor their charm without the crowds.

By now, you've discovered how Germany's scenic train routes allow you to soak up the country's diverse beauty while traveling sustainably.

Chapter 8: Local Insights and Tips

To truly make the most of your journey through Germany by train, it's important to go beyond the basics. This chapter provides insider knowledge about must-see attractions, cultural etiquette, and tools to enhance your travel experience. These tips will help you blend in like a local and navigate seamlessly.

8.1 Must-See Attractions in Each City

Germany's cities are packed with iconic landmarks, hidden gems, and unique experiences. Here's a curated list of must-see attractions for some of the country's top destinations:

Berlin
- Brandenburg Gate: A symbol of unity and history.
- Berlin Wall Memorial & East Side Gallery: Reflect on the city's divided past.
- Museum Island: A UNESCO World Heritage Site featuring five world-class museums.

- Tiergarten Park: Perfect for picnics or renting a paddleboat at the lake.

Munich
- Neuschwanstein Castle: Day trip to King Ludwig II's fairy-tale palace.
- Marienplatz: Admire the Glockenspiel clock tower and explore the historic square.
- English Garden: One of Europe's largest urban parks, complete with surfers and beer gardens.
- BMW Museum: A paradise for car enthusiasts.

Frankfurt
- Römer Square: Step back in time with half-timbered buildings.
- Main Tower: Panoramic views of the skyline and river.
- Städel Museum: Home to masterpieces spanning centuries.
- Palmengarten: A serene botanical garden perfect for relaxation.

Hamburg
- Elbphilharmonie: Modern architecture meets incredible acoustics.
- Speicherstadt: A UNESCO-listed warehouse district with canals and lights.

- Miniatur Wunderland: The world's largest model railway exhibit.
- Harbor Boat Tours: See the bustling port from the water.

Cologne
- Kölner Dom (Cologne Cathedral): Climb the towers for stunning views.
- Hohenzollern Bridge: Add a love lock and enjoy riverside views.
- Belgian Quarter: Trendy bars, cafes, and street art.
-Ludwig Museum: Contemporary art including works by Picasso.

Other Cities
- Düsseldorf: Königsallee shopping boulevard and Rheinturm TV Tower.
- Stuttgart: Mercedes-Benz and Porsche museums, Wilhelma Zoo.
- Leipzig: Bach Museum and vibrant arts scene in Plagwitz district.
- Nuremberg: Imperial Castle and Nazi Documentation Center.

Each city has its own personality, so mix famous landmarks with local recommendations to create a well-rounded itinerary.

8.2 Cultural Etiquette: What to Know Before You Go

Understanding German culture and customs will help you connect with locals and avoid awkward moments. Here's what you need to know:

Greetings and Politeness
- Germans value politeness. Always say "hello" (Guten Tag) when entering shops or restaurants and "thank you" (Danke) when leaving.
- Handshakes are common for formal introductions; close friends may hug or kiss cheeks.

Tipping
- Tipping is customary but modest. Round up your bill or leave 5–10% for good service.
- Say "Stimmt so" ("Keep the change") if you're happy with the tip amount already included.

Public Behavior
- Keep voices low in public spaces—loud conversations can be seen as impolite.
- Queuing is sacred. Always wait your turn patiently.

Dining Etiquette
- Wait to be seated unless signs indicate otherwise.

- Start meals by saying "Guten Appetit," and finish with "Danke, es war sehr lecker" (Thank you, it was very delicious).
- Don't start eating until everyone has been served.

Punctuality
- Germans take punctuality seriously. Arrive on time for appointments, trains, and social gatherings.

Recycling
- Recycling is a way of life in Germany. Dispose of trash in designated bins for paper, plastic, glass, and general waste.

Language Basics
While many Germans speak English, learning a few phrases shows respect:
- "Entschuldigung" – Excuse me / Sorry
- "Wo ist…?" – Where is…?
- "Wie viel kostet das?" – How much does this cost?

8.3 Helpful Apps and Resources for Travelers

Technology makes traveling easier than ever. Here are some apps and tools to simplify your train adventures in Germany:

Train Travel Apps

- DB Navigator: Official Deutsche Bahn app for booking tickets, checking schedules, and tracking delays.
- Omio (formerly GoEuro): Compare train, bus, and flight options across Europe.
- Trainline EU: Another great option for booking and managing rail journeys.

Navigation Tools

- Google Maps: Reliable for finding stations, walking directions, and nearby attractions.
- Citymapper: Ideal for navigating public transport within cities.

Accommodation and Dining

- Booking.com / Airbnb: Find hotels, hostels, or apartments.
- Yelp / Google Reviews: Discover local restaurants and read reviews.
- Too Good To Go: Rescue discounted food from bakeries and cafes to reduce waste.

Language Assistance

- Google Translate: Instant translations for signs, menus, and conversations.

- Duolingo: Learn basic German phrases before your trip.

Currency and Budgeting
- XE Currency Converter: Stay updated on exchange rates.
- Revolut / Wise: Manage international spending and avoid high bank fees.

Miscellaneous
- PackPoint: Create packing lists tailored to your destination and activities.
- TripIt: Organize all your bookings and itineraries in one place.
- Weather Apps (e.g., AccuWeather): Prepare for changing conditions during outdoor excursions.

With these insights and tools, you'll feel confident navigating Germany's cities and understanding its culture.

Chapter 9: Culinary Delights

Germany's food scene is as diverse as its landscapes, offering hearty meals, sweet treats, and refreshing beverages that reflect the country's rich traditions. Whether you're indulging in a sit-down meal or grabbing a quick bite at a train station, there's something for every palate. Let's explore the culinary highlights of Germany and discover what makes each region unique.

9.1 Traditional German Cuisine: What to Try

German cuisine is hearty, flavorful, and deeply rooted in history. Here are some must-try dishes:

Meat Dishes
- Bratwurst: A type of sausage grilled to perfection, often served with mustard and bread. Varieties include Nürnberger Bratwurst (smaller) and Thüringer Rostbratwurst (spicier).

- Schnitzel: Breaded and fried meat cutlets, typically made from pork or veal. Wiener Schnitzel is a classic Austrian-inspired version.
- Schweinshaxe: Roasted pork knuckle with crispy skin, usually served with sauerkraut and potato dumplings.
- Rouladen: Thin slices of beef rolled around bacon, onions, and pickles, then braised in gravy.

Side Dishes
- Spätzle: Soft egg noodles often paired with stews or topped with cheese (Käsespätzle).
- Kartoffelsalat (Potato Salad): A staple side dish, either vinegar-based or creamy, depending on the region.
- Sauerkraut: Fermented cabbage that adds tanginess to savory dishes.

Breads and Pastries
- Pretzels (Brezeln): Large, chewy knots of dough sprinkled with coarse salt. Look for regional variations like Laugenstangen (pretzel sticks).
- Stollen: A rich fruitcake traditionally enjoyed during Christmas markets.
-Black Forest Cake (Schwarzwälder Kirschtorte): Layers of chocolate sponge, whipped cream, and cherries soaked in kirsch liqueur.

Drinks
- Beer: Germany boasts over 5,000 breweries! Try wheat beer (Weißbier), pilsner (Pils), or smoked beer (Rauchbier) depending on the region.
- Glühwein: Mulled wine spiced with cinnamon, cloves, and citrus—perfect for winter markets.
- Apfelwein (Apple Wine): A specialty of Frankfurt and Hesse, similar to cider.

9.2 Street Food: Quick Bites on the Go

When you're rushing between trains or exploring busy stations, street food offers a convenient way to sample local flavors. Here are some quintessential German snacks:

Currywurst
- A Berlin-born classic, this dish consists of sliced bratwurst smothered in curry ketchup and sprinkled with curry powder. It's often served with fries or bread.

Döner Kebab
- Originating from Turkish immigrants, döner has become a beloved fast-food staple across Germany.

Thinly sliced meat is wrapped in flatbread with fresh veggies and sauces.

Brezeln und Würstchen
- Grab a soft pretzel paired with a small sausage for an authentic Bavarian snack. Many bakeries near train stations sell these.

Leberkäse
- Despite its name ("liver cheese"), this loaf isn't made from liver. It's a baked meatloaf sliced and served in rolls, popular in southern Germany.

Fischbrötchen
- Found especially in northern port cities like Hamburg, these fish sandwiches feature pickled herring, shrimp, or smoked salmon on crusty bread.

Pro Tip:
Look for food stalls inside major train stations like Munich Hauptbahnhof or Berlin Hauptbahnhof— they offer quick, affordable options without sacrificing quality.

9.3 Dining Experiences: Restaurants Near Train Stations

Train stations aren't just transit hubs—they're also home to fantastic eateries. Here are some dining recommendations near key stations:

Berlin Hauptbahnhof
- Café Haferkorn: Known for its cozy atmosphere and hearty German breakfasts.
- Zentraler Omnibusbahnhof (ZOB): Adjacent to the station, this area has international restaurants catering to travelers.

Munich Hauptbahnhof
- Hofbräu München: A branch of the famous Hofbräuhaus brewery, offering traditional Bavarian fare right at the station.
- Paulaner am Bahnhof: Enjoy freshly brewed beer and schnitzel while waiting for your train.

Frankfurt Hauptbahnhof
- Emil's Café & Bar: Perfect for coffee, cakes, or light meals in a stylish setting.
- Vapiano: Casual Italian dining with fresh pasta and pizza.

Hamburg Hauptbahnhof
- Hamburger Bahnhof Restaurant: Classic German dishes with a modern twist.
-Asia Imbiss Sticks'n'Sushi: For those craving Asian fusion, this spot serves sushi and noodle bowls.

Cologne Hauptbahnhof
- Brauerei zur Malzmühle: Sample Kölsch beer and regional specialties steps away from the cathedral.
- Food Courts: The station has multiple food courts offering everything from burgers to vegan wraps.

Pro Tip:
Check opening hours ahead of time, as some restaurants may close earlier than expected on Sundays or holidays.

9.4 Unique Local Treats from Each Region

Germany's regions take pride in their distinct culinary traditions. Here's a guide to sampling local specialties:

Bavaria
- Weißwurst: A white sausage made from veal, typically eaten before noon with sweet mustard and pretzels.

- Obatzda: A creamy cheese spread flavored with paprika, perfect with bread and radishes.

Baden-Württemberg
- Maultaschen: Pasta pockets filled with meat, spinach, or cheese, similar to ravioli but larger.
- Flammkuchen: A thin, crispy tart topped with crème fraîche, onions, and bacon.

Rhine Valley
- Riesling Wine: Sip crisp white wines grown in terraced vineyards along the Rhine River.
- Handkäse mit Musik: A marinated cheese dish native to Frankfurt, often served with vinegar and oil dressing.

North Germany
- Labskaus: A sailor-inspired dish made from corned beef, beets, potatoes, and herring, served with pickles and eggs.
- Rote Grütze: A red berry pudding typically paired with vanilla sauce.

East Germany
- Soljanka: A hearty soup originating from Eastern Europe, featuring meats, vegetables, and spices.
- Quarkkeulchen: Potato pancakes mixed with quark (a soft cheese) and served with applesauce.

Ruhr Area
- Pfefferpotthast: A slow-cooked beef stew seasoned with pepper and juniper berries, typical of the region.
- Halve Hahn: Not actually half a chicken but rather a rye bread roll topped with Gouda cheese, butter, and pickles.

With these culinary insights, you'll never go hungry while traveling through Germany by train.

Chapter 10: Onboard Experience

Traveling by train in Germany isn't just about getting from point A to point B—it's about enjoying the journey itself. From comfortable seating to onboard dining and breathtaking views, German trains are designed to make your trip as pleasant as possible. In this chapter, we'll explore what you can expect during your ride and how to maximize your onboard experience.

10.1 Comfort and Amenities: What Each Class Offers

Deutsche Bahn (DB) offers two main classes of service on its trains: Second Class and First Class. Here's a breakdown of what each class provides:

Second Class (Standard)
- Seating: Spacious enough for most travelers, with rows typically configured in pairs or groups of four.
- Comfort: Adjustable headrests, fold-down tables, and ample legroom.

- Best For: Budget-conscious travelers who prioritize affordability over luxury.
- Extras: Quiet zones available on many trains for those seeking peace and quiet.

First Class
- Seating: Larger seats with more recline and extra space between rows.
- Comfort: Plusher upholstery, dedicated reading lights, and quieter cabins.
- Perks: Complimentary newspapers, snacks, and beverages on long-distance ICE trains.
-Best For: Business travelers, couples celebrating special occasions, or anyone looking for an upgraded experience.

Special Features Across Classes
- Bike Racks: Many regional trains have designated areas for bicycles.
- Family-Friendly Cars: Some trains include play areas or family compartments.
- Accessibility: Wheelchair-accessible cars and priority seating for elderly or disabled passengers.

Pro Tip:
If you're traveling long distances, consider reserving a seat near the window for better views—especially on scenic routes like the Rhine Valley or Bavarian Alps.

10.2 Dining Options: Food and Drink on Trains

While shorter trips may not include full dining services, long-distance ICE trains often provide food and drink options right at your seat. Here's what to expect:

Onboard Cafés/Bistros
- Found on most ICE and some IC trains, these cafés serve hot meals, sandwiches, salads, coffee, beer, wine, and soft drinks.
- Popular items include:
- Warm pretzels and hearty sandwiches.
- Schnitzel baguettes or vegetarian wraps.
- Desserts like apple strudel or Black Forest cake slices.

Trolley Service
- Attendants push trolleys through the train offering snacks, beverages, and light meals.
- Great for grabbing quick refreshments without leaving your seat.

BYO (Bring Your Own)

- Regional trains (RE/RB) and S-Bahns don't usually have dining cars, so bringing your own food is a smart idea.
- Pick up fresh baked goods, sandwiches, or fruit at train station bakeries before boarding.

Pro Tip:
Download the DB app ahead of time to pre-order meals directly to your seat on select ICE trains—a convenient way to avoid lines.

10.3 Staying Entertained: Wi-Fi and Charging Outlets

Modern German trains come equipped with amenities to keep you connected and entertained throughout your journey.

Wi-Fi Access
- Free Wi-Fi is available on all ICE trains and many regional trains. Simply connect to "WIFIonICE" using your device.
- Speed varies depending on signal strength but is generally sufficient for browsing, streaming, or working online.

Charging Outlets
- Power outlets are located under seats or next to tables on newer ICE trains.
- While older trains might lack outlets, USB ports are becoming increasingly common.

Entertainment Ideas
- **Movies/Shows: Download episodes or movies onto your tablet or laptop before boarding.**
- **Books/Audiobooks: Bring a Kindle or e-reader for hours of distraction-free reading.**
- **Music/Podcasts: Curate playlists or queue up podcast episodes for background entertainment.**
- **Games: Travel-sized board games or apps can be fun if you're traveling with companions.**

Pro Tip:
Use the downtime to journal your adventures or plan your next destination—you'd be surprised how much inspiration strikes while watching the scenery roll by!

10.4 Making the Most of Your Journey: Scenic Views and Stops

One of the greatest joys of train travel is soaking in the stunning landscapes along the way. Here's how to make the most of your scenic journey:

Choose Window Seats
- Always opt for a window seat when booking tickets or hopping on board last-minute.
- Keep your camera or phone handy to capture picturesque moments.

Scenic Routes Worth Booking
- Rhine Valley Line: Vineyards, castles, and riverside towns create postcard-perfect views.
- Bavarian Alps Route: Snow-capped peaks and alpine villages will leave you awestruck.
- Black Forest Railway: Dense forests, sparkling streams, and quaint villages feel magical.
- Harz Mountains Narrow-Gauge Railway: Steam-powered trains wind through dramatic gorges and forests.

Short Breaks Along the Way
- If time permits, consider breaking your journey to explore small towns en route.
- Example: Stop in Rüdesheim on the Rhine Valley line for wine tasting or Bacharach for a riverside stroll.

Interactive Experiences

- Use audio guides or apps like Rick Steves' Europe to learn about landmarks visible from the train.
- Engage with fellow passengers—Germans are often friendly and happy to share stories about their hometowns.

Pro Tip:
Pack binoculars for wildlife spotting or closer looks at distant castles and mountain ranges.

By now, you should feel ready to settle into your seat and embrace the magic of train travel in Germany.

Chapter 11: Transportation Beyond the Train

While trains are the backbone of your German adventure, there's a whole world of transportation options waiting to help you explore cities, towns, and even neighboring countries. This chapter will guide you through local public transport, bike rentals, taxis, and day trips so you can seamlessly continue your journey once you step off the train.

11.1 Local Public Transport: Buses, Trams, and Subways

Germany's cities boast some of the most efficient and well-connected public transport systems in the world. Whether you're hopping between neighborhoods or heading out for a day of sightseeing, buses, trams, and subways (known as U-Bahn and S-Bahn) are your best friends.

Types of Local Transport

- Buses: Perfect for reaching areas not covered by trains or trams. They're especially useful in smaller towns.
- Trams: Street-level trains that weave through city centers. Look for them in cities like Berlin, Munich, and Leipzig.
- Subways (U-Bahn): Underground trains ideal for quick commutes within urban areas.
- City Trains (S-Bahn): Overground trains connecting suburbs to city centers. Think of them as mini-trains for shorter distances.

How It Works
- Tickets and Zones: Most cities use zone-based pricing. Buy tickets at machines, kiosks, or via apps like DB Navigator. Validate your ticket before boarding!
- Day Passes: If you plan to explore all day, consider purchasing a day pass—it's often cheaper than buying multiple single rides.
- Transfers: One ticket usually covers transfers across buses, trams, and subways within a set time frame.

Tips for First-Timers
- Always check if your hotel or accommodation offers discounted transit passes.
- Keep an eye on signs indicating which platform or stop to use—most are clearly marked in English.

- Be mindful of quiet zones on trams and subways; Germans value peace and quiet during their commutes.

With these tools, navigating any German city becomes a breeze!

11.2 Renting Bikes and E-Scooters for City Exploration

Germany is incredibly bike-friendly, with dedicated cycling lanes in almost every city. Renting a bike or e-scooter is a fantastic way to see more while staying active.

Why Choose a Bike or E-Scooter?
- Flexibility: Explore narrow streets, parks, and scenic routes that aren't accessible by car or public transport.
- Eco-Friendly: Zero emissions mean you're doing your part for the environment.
- Fun Factor: Pedaling along riverside paths or cruising through historic districts adds a unique charm to your trip.

Where to Rent

- Bike Rentals: Many train stations have rental shops, and companies like Nextbike and Call a Bike operate nationwide. Simply download their app, unlock a bike, and start riding.
- E-Scooters: Popular services like Lime, Tier, and Bird operate in major cities. Use their apps to locate scooters nearby.

Rules of the Road
- Stick to designated bike lanes whenever possible.
- Helmets aren't mandatory but are highly recommended.
- Respect pedestrian areas and avoid riding on sidewalks unless specified.

Pro Tip: Some cities offer guided bike tours—a great way to learn about local history while getting exercise!

11.3 Taxis and Ride-Sharing Services: Getting Around

Sometimes convenience outweighs cost, and that's where taxis and ride-sharing services come in handy.

Taxis

- Hailing a Taxi: You can flag down taxis on the street in larger cities, though it's more common to find them at stands near train stations or airports.
- Booking Ahead: Use apps like MyTaxi (now FREE NOW) to book and track your ride.
- Costs: Taxis are metered, with base fares starting around €3–€4, plus additional charges per kilometer. Late-night rides may incur higher fees.

Ride-Sharing Services
- Uber and Bolt: Available in select cities, these platforms work similarly to what you might be used to back home.
- Local Alternatives: Companies like Kapten and MOIA cater to shared rides, making them budget-friendly options.

When to Use Them
- Late-night travel when public transport isn't running.
- Traveling with heavy luggage or mobility issues.
- Heading to places without good public transport connections.

While pricier than buses or trains, taxis and ride-shares provide comfort and reliability when you need it most.

11.4 Day Trips: Expanding Your Travel Horizons

Train travel opens up endless possibilities for day trips from major hubs. Here are some ideas to inspire your wanderlust:

From Berlin
- Potsdam: Visit Sanssouci Palace and stroll through its lush gardens (30 minutes by train).
- Leipzig: Discover this vibrant cultural hub known for its music and art scene (1.5 hours by train).

From Munich
- Neuschwanstein Castle: Step into a fairytale at King Ludwig II's iconic castle (2 hours by train + shuttle).
-Garmisch-Partenkirchen: Hike in the Bavarian Alps or visit Zugspitze, Germany's highest peak (1.5 hours by train).

From Frankfurt
- Heidelberg: Wander cobblestone streets and admire the ruins of Heidelberg Castle (1 hour by train).
- Rhine Valley: Cruise past castles and vineyards along the Rhine River (1–2 hours by train).

From Hamburg

- Lübeck: Sample marzipan and marvel at medieval architecture (45 minutes by train).
- Sylt Island: Relax on sandy beaches or try windsurfing (3 hours by train + ferry).

Planning Your Day Trip
- Check train schedules ahead of time to maximize your day.
- Pack snacks, water, and a small backpack for essentials.
- Consider guided tours if you want deeper insights into your destination.

Day trips let you experience even more of Germany's diversity without straying too far from your main itinerary.

By combining trains with local transport, bikes, taxis, and day trips, you'll have all the tools you need to explore every corner of Germany. Now go forth and discover the magic beyond the rails!

Chapter 12: Accommodation Options Near Train Stations

After a long day of train travel, you'll want a comfortable place to rest your head. Fortunately, Germany offers a wide range of accommodations near train stations, ensuring convenience and variety for every type of traveler. In this chapter, we'll explore hotels, hostels, guesthouses, and short-term rentals, along with tips for booking the perfect stay.

12.1 Hotels: Recommendations for Every Budget

Hotels are a classic choice for travelers seeking comfort, service, and proximity to train stations. Whether you're splurging on luxury or sticking to a budget, there's something for everyone.

Luxury Hotels
- **Example: Steigenberger Hotel am Kölner Dom (Cologne)**
- **Price per Night: €250–€400**

- Amenities: Free Wi-Fi, spa, fitness center, restaurant, concierge service
- Working Hours: Check-in: 3 PM, Check-out: 12 PM
- Number of Guests per Room: 2–4 (family rooms available)
- Address: Bahnhofsvorplatz 1, 50667 Cologne

- Why Stay Here? This hotel is steps away from Cologne Cathedral and the main train station, making it perfect for sightseeing. The luxurious amenities and stunning views make it worth the splurge.

Mid-Range Hotels
- Example: Novum Hotel Königshof Hamburg am Hauptbahnhof (Hamburg)
- Price per Night: €100–€180
- Amenities: Free Wi-Fi, breakfast buffet, lounge area, 24-hour reception
- Working Hours: Check-in: 2 PM, Check-out: 11 AM
- Number of Guests per Room: 2–3
- Address: Kirchenallee 41, 20099 Hamburg

- Why Stay Here? Located directly across from Hamburg's main train station, this hotel is ideal for business and leisure travelers alike. The clean rooms and friendly staff ensure a pleasant stay.

Budget Hotels

- Example: ibis Styles Frankfurt City (Frankfurt)
- Price per Night: €60–€100
-Amenities: Free Wi-Fi, complimentary breakfast, air conditioning
- Working Hours: Check-in: 3 PM, Check-out: 12 PM
- Number of Guests per Room: 2–3
- Address: Poststraße 18, 60329 Frankfurt

- Why Stay Here? Affordable yet stylish, this hotel is just a 5-minute walk from Frankfurt Hauptbahnhof. It's perfect for solo travelers or couples looking for value without compromising quality.

12.2 Hostels and Guesthouses: Affordable Stays

For budget-conscious travelers or those seeking a social atmosphere, hostels and guesthouses are excellent options.

Hostels
- Example: Generator Berlin Mitte (Berlin)
- Price per Night: Dorm beds: €20–€40; Private rooms: €60–€90
- Amenities: Free Wi-Fi, communal kitchen, bar, bike rentals, 24-hour reception

- Working Hours: Open 24/7
- Number of Guests per Room: Dorms: 4–10; Private rooms: 2–3
- Address: Oranienburger Straße 65, 10117 Berlin

- Why Stay Here? This trendy hostel combines affordability with a vibrant social scene. Its central location near Berlin Nordbahnhof makes it easy to explore the city.

Guesthouses
- Example: Pension am Roßmarkt (Munich)
- Price per Night: €50–€80
- Amenities: Free Wi-Fi, shared kitchen, daily housekeeping
- Working Hours: Check-in: 2 PM, Check-out: 11 AM
- Number of Guests per Room: 2–3
- Address: Rosenstraße 1, 80331 Munich

- Why Stay Here? A cozy guesthouse located a short walk from Munich Hauptbahnhof, offering a homely vibe and personalized service at an unbeatable price.

12.3 Short-Term Rentals: Finding Your Home Away from Home

Short-term rentals through platforms like Airbnb or Booking.com provide flexibility and independence, especially for families or groups.

Studio Apartment Example
- Example: Modern Studio Near Stuttgart Central Station (Stuttgart)
- Price per Night: €40–€70
- Amenities: Kitchenette, free Wi-Fi, TV, washing machine
- Working Hours: Self-check-in via keybox; check-out by 10 AM
- Number of Guests per Room: 1–2
- Address: Königstraße 10, 70173 Stuttgart

- Why Stay Here? Compact and affordable, this studio is perfect for solo travelers or couples who prefer cooking their own meals.

Family-Friendly Apartment
- Example: Spacious 2-Bedroom Apartment in Dresden Neustadt (Dresden)
- Price per Night: €80–€120
-Amenities: Fully equipped kitchen, free Wi-Fi, balcony, parking space
- Working Hours: Check-in: 3 PM, Check-out: 11 AM
- Number of Guests per Room: Up to 5
- Address: Bautzner Straße 30, 01099 Dresden

- Why Stay Here? Ideal for families or small groups, this apartment offers ample space and proximity to Dresden's cultural attractions, just a 10-minute tram ride from the train station.

12.4 Tips for Booking Accommodations

Booking the right accommodation can make or break your trip. Follow these tips to secure the best deal:

1. Book Early
- Popular locations near train stations fill up quickly, especially during peak seasons like summer or Christmas markets. Reserve your stay at least 2–3 months in advance.

2. Use Comparison Websites
- Platforms like Booking.com, Expedia, and Airbnb allow you to compare prices, read reviews, and filter results based on your preferences.

3. Look for Discounts
- Many hotels offer "early bird" rates or last-minute deals. Sign up for newsletters or loyalty programs to access exclusive promotions.

4. Check Location Carefully
- Proximity to the train station is convenient, but noisy areas may affect your sleep. Read reviews to gauge noise levels and safety.

5. Understand Cancellation Policies
-Life happens! Always choose accommodations with flexible cancellation policies, especially if your travel plans might change.

6. Consider Amenities
- Prioritize what matters most to you—free breakfast, Wi-Fi, or a gym—and factor that into your decision.

By following these guidelines, you'll find the perfect place to rest and recharge after a day of exploring Germany by train.

Germany's diverse accommodation options ensure that no matter your budget or style, you'll always have a welcoming place to call home during your travels.

Chapter 13: Local Insights and Tips

Germany is a treasure trove of history, culture, and natural beauty. To make the most of your journey, it's important to know the must-see attractions, understand cultural norms, and arm yourself with helpful tools and apps. This chapter will provide insider knowledge to enhance your travel experience.

13.1 Must-See Attractions in Each City

Germany's cities are each unique, offering a mix of iconic landmarks, hidden gems, and unforgettable experiences. Here's a curated list of must-see attractions:

Berlin
- Brandenburg Gate: A symbol of unity and history, this neoclassical monument is a must-visit.
- Berlin Wall Memorial: Learn about the Cold War era at this poignant site.
- Museum Island: A UNESCO World Heritage Site featuring five world-class museums.

Munich
- Marienplatz: The heart of Munich, home to the famous Glockenspiel clock tower.
- Neuschwanstein Castle: A fairytale castle nestled in the Bavarian Alps (a short train ride away).
- English Garden: One of Europe's largest urban parks, perfect for picnics or paddle boating.

Hamburg
- Elbphilharmonie: A stunning concert hall with breathtaking views of the harbor.
- Speicherstadt: A historic warehouse district turned UNESCO World Heritage Site.
- St. Michaelis Church: Climb the tower for panoramic views of the city.

Cologne
- Cologne Cathedral (Kölner Dom): A Gothic masterpiece and one of Germany's most iconic landmarks.
- Hohenzollern Bridge Love Locks: Add your own lock to this romantic tradition.
- Chocolate Museum: Indulge in Germany's sweet side.

Frankfurt
- Römer Square: Admire Frankfurt's medieval charm and colorful half-timbered houses.

- Main Tower: Enjoy sweeping views of the skyline from this observation deck.
- Palmengarten: A serene botanical garden ideal for a relaxing afternoon.

Smaller Gems
- Heidelberg: Explore the ruins of Heidelberg Castle and stroll along the Neckar River.
- Rothenburg ob der Tauber: Step into a storybook town with cobblestone streets and medieval architecture.
- Bamberg: Discover its UNESCO-listed old town and sample smoked beer at local breweries.

Pro Tip: Many attractions offer guided tours or audio guides—check ahead to see if they're available in English!

13.2 Cultural Etiquette: What to Know Before You Go

Germans value politeness, punctuality, and respect for rules. Understanding these cultural norms will help you blend in and avoid unintentional faux pas.

Greetings

- Shake hands firmly when meeting someone new.
- Use formal titles like "Herr" (Mr.) or "Frau" (Mrs./Ms.) unless invited to use first names.

Tipping
- Tipping is customary but not mandatory. Round up your bill or leave 5–10% for good service.
- For example, if your meal costs €22, leaving €25 is polite.

Public Behavior
- Keep your voice down on public transport and in quiet zones.
- Always validate your ticket before boarding buses, trams, or trains.

Recycling
- Germans take recycling seriously. Look for separate bins for plastic, glass, paper, and general waste.

Punctuality
- Being late is considered rude. Arrive on time for appointments, meetings, or even casual meetups.

Personal Space
- Respect personal boundaries; don't stand too close or touch people unnecessarily.

Understanding these customs will show locals that you're thoughtful and respectful—a great way to create positive impressions!

13.3 Helpful Apps and Resources for Travelers

Technology makes travel easier than ever. These apps and resources will keep you informed, connected, and prepared throughout your trip.

Transportation Apps
- DB Navigator: Plan train journeys, check schedules, and book tickets.
-City-Specific Transit Apps: Examples include BVG (Berlin), MVV (Munich), and HVV (Hamburg) for local transport.

Accommodation Booking
- Booking.com: Compare hotels, hostels, and guesthouses.
- Airbnb: Find short-term rentals and unique stays.

Food and Dining
- Yelp/EatOut: Search for restaurants and read reviews.

- Too Good To Go: Save money by purchasing surplus food from cafes and bakeries at discounted prices.

Navigation
- Google Maps: Essential for navigating cities, finding attractions, and estimating travel times.
- Maps.me: Download offline maps for areas without internet access.

Language Assistance
- Google Translate: Translate text, signs, and conversations in real-time.
- Duolingo: Learn basic German phrases before your trip.

Other Useful Tools
- XE Currency Converter: Stay updated on exchange rates.
- PackPoint: Create packing lists tailored to your destination and activities.
- Weather Apps: Use AccuWeather or BBC Weather to plan around seasonal conditions.

Bonus Tip: Carry a portable charger! Train stations and tourist spots often have limited outlets, so staying powered up is crucial.

With these local insights and practical tips, you'll feel confident exploring Germany's vibrant cities and charming countryside. From knowing where to go to understanding how to behave, this chapter equips you with everything you need to immerse yourself in the German experience.

Chapter 14: Traveler Stories and Testimonials

There's nothing quite like hearing from others who have walked—or rather, ridden—the same tracks. In this chapter, we'll share inspiring stories, lessons learned, and reflections from travelers who explored Germany by train. These firsthand accounts will motivate you, offer practical advice, and remind you why train travel is such a transformative experience.

14.1 Inspiring Stories from Fellow Travelers

Story 1: A Solo Journey of Self-Discovery
By Sarah T., USA
"I'd always dreamed of visiting Europe, but the idea of navigating foreign cities alone felt overwhelming. Then I discovered Germany's train system—it was so easy! Starting in Berlin, I took an ICE train to Dresden, then hopped on regional lines to explore smaller towns like Meissen and Pirna. One of my favorite moments was sitting by the Elbe River after a day of sightseeing, feeling completely at peace. The

trains gave me freedom without sacrificing comfort. By the end of my trip, I realized how much confidence I'd gained just by trusting myself to figure things out."

Key Takeaway: Train travel empowers solo adventurers to explore independently while staying connected to a reliable network.

Story 2: Family Adventures Across Bavaria
By Rajiv K., India
"My family and I decided to spend two weeks exploring Bavaria by train. We started in Munich, where we stayed near the Hauptbahnhof, then took day trips to Neuschwanstein Castle, Garmisch-Partenkirchen, and Salzburg. The kids loved riding the trains—they thought it was like being in a movie! What stood out most was how stress-free everything felt. No need to worry about parking or rental cars; we could simply sit back and enjoy the scenery. It brought us closer together as a family."

Key Takeaway: Trains are perfect for families, offering convenience and opportunities to bond over shared experiences.

Story 3: Romance on the Rails
By Emily R., UK

"My partner and I wanted our anniversary trip to be special, so we planned a romantic rail journey through the Rhine Valley. We booked a scenic route that stopped in Koblenz, Rüdesheim, and Bacharach. Watching vineyards roll past our window while sipping local wine made us feel like characters in a novel. At each stop, we wandered cobblestone streets hand-in-hand, discovering hidden cafés and medieval castles. It wasn't just a vacation—it was pure magic."

Key Takeaway: Train journeys create unforgettable memories, especially for couples seeking intimacy and adventure.

14.2 Lessons Learned: Common Challenges and Solutions

Even the best-laid plans can encounter hiccups. Here are some common challenges travelers face when exploring Germany by train—and how to overcome them.

Challenge 1: Language Barriers
While many Germans speak English, not all signs or announcements are translated.

Solution:
- Use apps like Google Translate to decipher unfamiliar words.
-Learn key phrases like "Wo ist der Bahnsteig?" (Where is the platform?) and "Wie viel kostet das?" (How much does this cost?).

Real-Life Example:
Mark, a Canadian traveler, once missed his stop because he didn't recognize the German name of his destination. He now keeps screenshots of station names handy to avoid confusion.

Challenge 2: Delays and Cancellations
Train delays happen occasionally, even in Germany's efficient system.

Solution:
- Check DB Navigator regularly for updates.
- Keep snacks, water, and entertainment (like books or podcasts) in your bag for unexpected waits.
- If your connection is missed due to a delay, ask staff for assistance—they'll help rebook your ticket.

Real-Life Example:
Lena, a frequent traveler, recalls a 90-minute delay caused by heavy snow. She used the time to chat with fellow passengers and ended up making lifelong

friends. "Sometimes disruptions lead to unexpected joys," she says.

Challenge 3: Overpacking
Carrying too much luggage can make train travel cumbersome.

Solution:
- Pack light and focus on versatile clothing.
- Invest in collapsible bags or packing cubes to maximize space.
- Leave room for souvenirs!

Real-Life Example:
Tom, an Australian backpacker, initially brought a bulky suitcase but switched to a carry-on halfway through his trip. "Traveling light changed my entire perspective," he admits. "I moved faster and felt freer."

14.3 How Train Travel Transformed Their Experience

Beyond convenience, train travel has a way of enriching journeys in profound ways. Here's what travelers say about how it transformed their trips:

Freedom to Explore

Many describe the flexibility of train travel as liberating. Unlike rigid flight schedules or complicated road maps, trains allow spontaneous detours.

- "We were heading to Cologne but decided to get off early in Bonn instead. We stumbled upon Beethoven's birthplace and spent hours wandering its charming streets." — Anna, Brazil

Connection to Nature

Trains offer unparalleled access to Germany's stunning landscapes, from forests to riversides.

- "The Black Forest Railway felt like stepping into a postcard. Every bend revealed another breathtaking view. It reminded me to slow down and appreciate the little things." — Hiroshi, Japan

Cultural Immersion

Sharing a train with locals provides authentic glimpses into daily life.

- "On the way to Hamburg, I struck up a conversation with a retired teacher who recommended her favorite coffee shop. Visiting later felt like finding a secret gem." — Chloe, Australia

Sustainability Matters
For eco-conscious travelers, choosing trains aligns with their values.

- "Knowing I was reducing my carbon footprint made the journey even more meaningful. Plus, seeing solar panels along the tracks inspired me to live greener back home." — Sophie, Canada

These stories and insights prove that train travel isn't just a mode of transportation—it's an integral part of the adventure itself. Whether you're seeking inspiration, practical advice, or reminders of why you chose this path, these testimonials show that the magic of Germany truly unfolds aboard its rails.

Chapter 15: Appendices

The appendices are designed to be your quick-reference guide for all things related to train travel in Germany. Whether you're looking up unfamiliar terms, brushing up on local phrases, or finding emergency contacts, this section has everything you need at your fingertips.

15.1 Glossary of Terms

Here's a list of general travel-related terms that will help you navigate your journey:

- Itinerary: A planned route or schedule for your trip.
- Hub: A central location where multiple transportation routes converge (e.g., major train stations).
- Pass: A document granting access to unlimited travel within specified limits (e.g., German Rail Pass).
- Zone-Based Pricing: Ticket costs determined by zones or regions covered during travel.
- Validation: The process of stamping your ticket before boarding to mark its start time.

15.2 Glossary of Train and Rail Terminology

To make sense of Germany's rail system, here's a breakdown of key terms:

Train Types
- ICE (InterCity Express): High-speed trains connecting major cities.
- IC (InterCity): Long-distance trains, slightly slower than ICE.
- RE (Regional Express): Regional trains stopping only at larger towns.
- RB (Regionalbahn): Local trains serving smaller stations.
- S-Bahn: City and suburban trains operating within metropolitan areas.

Station Terms
- Hauptbahnhof (Hbf): Main train station.
- Bahnsteig: Platform.
- Ausgang: Exit.
- Gleis: Track number.
- Fahrkarte: Ticket.

Ticketing Terms

- Bahncard: A discount card offering reduced fares on DB tickets.
- Flexpreis: Flexible fare allowing free changes and cancellations.
- Sparpreis: Discounted fare with limited flexibility.
- Gruppenticket: Group ticket for discounted group travel.

15.3 Glossary of Local Phrases

Brushing up on basic German phrases can go a long way in making your trip smoother:

Greetings and Politeness
- Hallo: Hello.
- Guten Tag: Good day.
- Bitte: Please / You're welcome.
- Danke: Thank you.
- Entschuldigung: Excuse me / Sorry.

At the Station
- Wo ist der Bahnsteig? Where is the platform?
- Wann fährt der Zug nach [destination]? When does the train to [destination] leave?
- Ich habe mich verlaufen. I'm lost.
- Wie viel kostet das? How much does this cost?

On the Train
- **Ist dies der richtige Zug nach [destination]? Is this the correct train to [destination]?**
- **Können Sie mir helfen? Can you help me?**
- **Stoppt dieser Zug in [station name]? Does this train stop at [station name]?**

15.4 Useful Contacts and Websites

These resources will help you plan, troubleshoot, and enhance your trip:

Official Websites
-
DeutscheBahn(DB):www.bahn.com – Official site for booking tickets and checking schedules.
-German National Tourist Board: www.germany.travel – Information on attractions and events.

Apps
- **DB Navigator: For real-time train updates and bookings.**

- Google Maps: Navigation and locating nearby amenities.
- Too Good To Go: Finding discounted food from local vendors.

Tourism Offices

-

BerlinTourismOffice:www.visitberlin.de

-

MunichTourismOffice:www.muenchen.de
-CologneTourismOffice:www.cologne-tourism.com

15.5 Emergency Contact Numbers
In case of emergencies, keep these numbers handy:

- General Emergency: 112 (works for medical, fire, and police assistance).
- Police Non-Emergency: 110.
- Deutsche Bahn Customer Service: +49 180 6 996633 (available 24/7).
- Lost Property Office (DB): +49 69 265 1055.

15.6 FAQ About Train Travel in Germany

Here are answers to some frequently asked questions:

Q: Do I need to reserve seats on German trains?
A: Reservations are optional for most regional trains but recommended for high-speed ICE trains during peak times. Some discounted tickets (e.g., Sparpreis) require reservations.

Q: Can I bring my pet on the train?
A: Yes, small pets travel free in carriers, while larger animals require a reduced fare ticket.

High season typically runs from June to August and December (Christmas markets). Shoulder seasons (April–May, September–October) are less crowded but still pleasant.

Q: What happens if I miss my connection due to a delay?
A: If your initial train is delayed, DB staff will assist in rebooking your ticket or refunding it. Keep your original ticket as proof.

Q: Are snacks and drinks available onboard?
A: Most ICE trains have dining cars or snack carts. Bring your own supplies for shorter regional journeys.

15.7 Recommended Reading and Resources

Expand your knowledge with these books, blogs, and guides:

Books

- Rick Steves Germany: A comprehensive guide to German culture, history, and travel tips.
- Lonely Planet Germany: Detailed insights into cities, attractions, and practical advice.
- All Aboard! The Complete Guide to Train Travel in Europe: Focuses on European rail systems, including Germany.

Blogs and Websites

- The Culture Trip: Articles on hidden gems and cultural experiences in Germany.
- Hand Luggage Only: Travel photography and tips for exploring Europe sustainably.
- Seat61: Expert advice on train travel across Europe, including detailed info on German routes.

Documentaries and Films

- Germany's Great Train Journeys: A BBC documentary showcasing scenic rail routes.
- The Lives of Others: A gripping film set in East Berlin, offering historical context.

With these appendices, you'll have all the tools you need to confidently navigate Germany by train. From decoding terminology to handling emergencies, this chapter ensures you're prepared for every step of the journey.

Chapter 16: Index

This index is designed to help you quickly locate specific topics, terms, or sections within this guide. Whether you're looking for practical advice, cultural insights, or destination details, the alphabetical organization ensures ease of navigation.

Use this index as a roadmap to revisit key sections or clarify any doubts as you plan and commence on your German train adventure. Happy travel!

Chapter 17: Conclusion: Bon Voyage—Your Journey Awaits

Congratulations! You've reached the final stop on this literary journey through Germany by train. From understanding the intricacies of Deutsche Bahn to uncovering hidden gems in charming towns, you now have all the tools you need to commence on an unforgettable adventure. But before you pack your bags and grab your ticket, let's take a moment to reflect on what makes train travel in Germany so special—and why it's more than just a mode of transportation.

Why Germany by Train?
Traveling by train is not merely about getting from point A to point B; it's about embracing the journey itself. As you glide past vineyard-dotted hills, medieval castles, and bustling cityscapes, you'll find yourself immersed in the beauty and diversity of Germany. Trains offer freedom, flexibility, and sustainability—a chance to slow down, connect with fellow travelers, and truly savor the landscapes that unfold outside your window.

Germany's rail system is a testament to efficiency, innovation, and accessibility. Whether you're exploring world-famous landmarks like Cologne Cathedral or wandering cobblestone streets in quaint villages like Rothenburg ob der Tauber, trains will be your gateway to discovery. And when combined with local transport, bike rentals, or day trips, they provide endless opportunities for exploration.

The Transformative Power of Travel

As we've seen through inspiring stories and testimonials, train travel has a way of transforming both journeys and people. It encourages spontaneity, fosters connections, and opens doors to new perspectives. For some, it's a solo voyage of self-discovery; for others, it's a family bonding experience or a romantic escape. Whatever your reason for traveling, one thing is certain: the memories you create aboard these rails will stay with you long after your trip ends.

A Final Word of Encouragement

Planning a trip can feel daunting, especially if you're venturing into unfamiliar territory. But remember, every great journey begins with a single step—or in this case, a single boarding pass. Trust in the knowledge you've gained from this guide, but also leave room for serendipity. Some of the best moments come from unexpected detours, friendly conversations, or simply taking time to watch the world go by.

Germany is a country rich in history, culture, and natural wonders, and its train network allows you to experience it all at your own pace. So don't be afraid to dream big, explore boldly, and embrace the magic of discovery.

Your Next Steps
- Plan Your Trip: Use the practical tips, sample itineraries, and glossaries in this guide to craft your perfect itinerary.
- Stay Connected: Bookmark useful websites, download essential apps, and keep emergency contacts handy.
- Share Your Stories: Once you return home, share your experiences with friends, family, or online communities. Who knows—you might inspire someone else to hop aboard their own German train adventure!

Thank You for Joining Us
Writing this guide has been a labor of love, and I hope it serves as a trusted companion throughout your travels. My wish for you is that each train ride brings

joy, each destination sparks wonder, and each encounter leaves you enriched.

So here's to you—the curious traveler ready to explore Germany by rail. May your journey be smooth, your views breathtaking, and your heart full of stories to tell. All aboard—it's time to make memories!

Safe travels and happy adventures!

Printed in Dunstable, United Kingdom